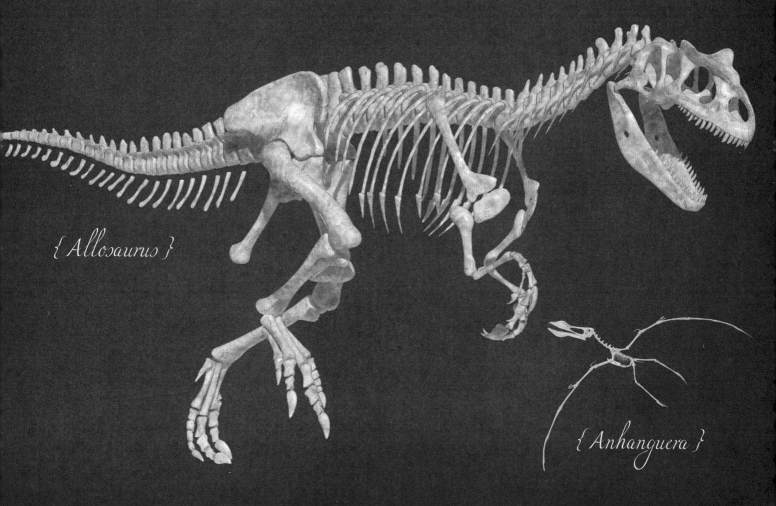

{ Diplodocus }

{ Opthalmosaurus }

{ Pachycephalosaurus }

Dinosaur Bones

{ Allosaurus }

{ Anhanguera }

A FIREFLY BOOK

Published by Firefly Books Ltd. 2016

Copyright © 2014 Marshall Editions

First printing

Publisher Cataloging-in-Publication Data (U.S.)

Colson, Rob, 1971-
Dinosaur bones : and what they tell us / Rob Colson.
[96] pages : illustrations ; cm.
Includes index.
Summary: "Fossils reveal much more about prehistoric animals and their world than you'd think. Everything we know about dinosaurs from their fossils is explained in this book with easy to follow facts and diagrams"
- Provided by publisher.
ISBN-13: 978-1-77085-717-9
ISBN-13: 978-1-77085-694-3 (paperback)
1. Dinosaurs - Juvenile literature. 2. Fossils - Juvenile literature. 3. Animals, Fossil - Juvenile literature. I. Title.
567.9 dc23 QE861.5C657 2016

Library and Archives Canada Cataloguing in Publication

Colson, Rob, 1971-, author
   Dinosaur bones : and what they tell us / Rob Colson.
Includes index.
ISBN-13: 978-1-77085-717-9
ISBN-13: 978-1-77085-694-3 (paperback)
   1. Dinosaurs--Juvenile literature. 2. Fossils--Juvenile literature. 3. Paleontology--Juvenile literature. I. Title.
QE861.5.C55 2016 j567.9 C2015-906165-2

Published in the United States by
Firefly Books (U.S.) Inc.
P.O. Box 1338, Ellicott Station
Buffalo, New York 14205

Published in Canada by
Firefly Books Ltd.
50 Staples Avenue, Unit 1
Richmond Hill, Ontario L4B 0A7

Printed in China

Conceived, designed, and produced by
Marshall Editions
Part of The Quarto Group
The Old Brewery
6 Blundell Street
London N7 9BH

Produced for Marshall Editions by Tall Tree Ltd.
Written by: Rob Colson
Illustrated by: Elizabeth Gray and Steve Kirk
Designed by: Malcolm Parchment, Sian Williams, and Jonathan Vipond
Consultant: Douglas Palmer

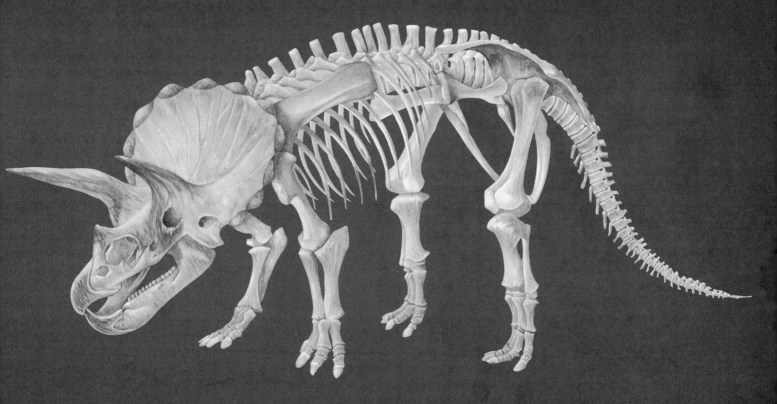

Dinosaur Bones

• • • ◦ ◦ ◦ ❖ ◦ ◦ ◦ • • •

And What They Tell Us

Rob Colson

FIREFLY BOOKS

CONTENTS

INTRODUCTION......................5

LIFE BEFORE THE DINOSAURS.......6-7

EARLY LAND ANIMALS..................8-9

ORNITHOLESTES.....................10-11

SMALL PREDATORS.....................12-13

GALLIMIMUS..........................14-15

OSTRICH DINOSAURS.....................16-17

DROMAEOSAURUS.......................18-19

DROMAEOSAURS.......................20-21

IGUANODON..........................22-23

IGUANODONTS........................24-25

LAMBEOSAURUS.......................26-27

DUCK-BILLED DINOSAURS........28-29

STEGOSAURUS........................30-31

PLATED DINOSAURS.....................32-33

TYRANNOSAURUS.......................34-35

TYRANNOSAURS.......................36-37

GIGANOTOSAURUS.....................38-39

GIANT PREDATORS.....................40-41

ALLOSAURUS........................42-43

EARLY PREDATORS.....................44-45

PSITTACOSAURUS.....................46-47

EARLY HORNED DINOSAURS....48-49

TRICERATOPS........................50-51

FRILLED DINOSAURS.....................52-53

ANKYLOSAURUS.....................54-55

ANKYLOSAURS.....................56-57

PACHYCEPHALOSAURUS............58-59

THICK-SKULLED DINOSAURS.....60-61

DIPLODOCUS........................62-63

LONG-NECKED DINOSAURS.....64-65

ANHANGUERA.....................66-67

FLYING REPTILES.....................68-69

OPHTHALMOSAURUS.................70-71

ICHTHYOSAURS.....................72-73

PLESIOSAURUS.....................74-75

PLESIOSAURS.....................76-77

ARCHAEOPTERYX.....................78-79

EARLY BIRDS.....................80-81

SMILODON.....................82-83

LARGE-TOOTHED HUNTERS....84-85

WOOLLY MAMMOTH.................86-87

MAMMOTHS AND
EARLY ELEPHANTS.....................88-89

TIMELINE.....................90-91

FOSSILS.....................92-93

GLOSSARY.....................94-95

INDEX.....................96

INTRODUCTION

{ Fig 1: Gastornis }

FOR 150 million years, life on our planet was dominated by huge reptiles. Dinosaurs roamed the land, while pterosaurs ruled the skies, and plesiosaurs and ichthyosaurs patrolled the oceans. Then, about 66 million years ago, all these giant animals disappeared, unable to cope with a sudden change in the climate. Other animals, such as birds and mammals, survived and took their place. We know about prehistoric animals from the remains they left behind as fossils. New fossils are being discovered all the time, changing how we think about these remarkable creatures. From fossils, scientists work out what the animals looked like and how they lived. Take a look at the bones of the dinosaurs and other prehistoric animals, and discover the latest ideas about how they lived and died.

{ Fig 2: Kronosaurus }

{ Fig 3: Ankylosaurus }

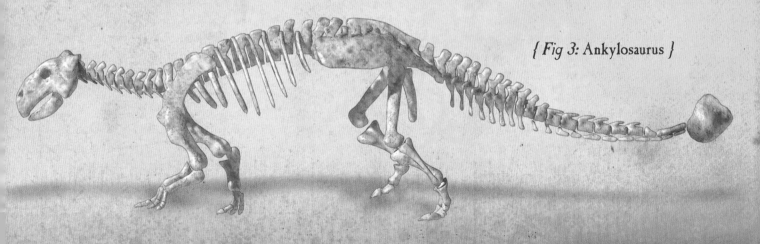

LIFE BEFORE THE DINOSAURS

LIFE on Earth began about 3.5 billion years ago. The first life forms were tiny single-celled microbes that lived in the warm oceans. For nearly 3 billion years, this was the only life on Earth. Then about 600 million years ago, multicelled life forms appeared, including the first animals.

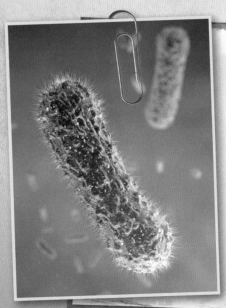

Bacteria

Single-celled bacteria are simple life forms, measuring up to just 5 microns long. Bacteria were among the first life to appear on Earth and are still the most common life form on the planet today.

EARLY FISH

The first fishlike creatures appeared about 500 million years ago. They were jawless and toothless fish known as agnathans.

Endoceras

Sacabambaspis

Strictoporella

Triarthrus

Coral

CAMBRIAN EXPLOSION

Many kinds of life appeared on Earth during an 80-million-year period starting 541 million years ago, called the Cambrian explosion. We still do not know why this explosion happened.

GIANT SEA HUNTERS

Sea scorpions first appeared in the oceans 400 million years ago. These predators could grow up to 6 ft (1.8 m) long.

TRILOBITE

Early in the Cambrian explosion, trilobites were seabed-dwelling creatures that became common in oceans all over the world. With their tough external shells and jointed limbs, trilobites were distant relatives of today's crabs and lobsters. More than 17,000 species of trilobite have been identified.

{ Fig 1: Fossil of a trilobite }

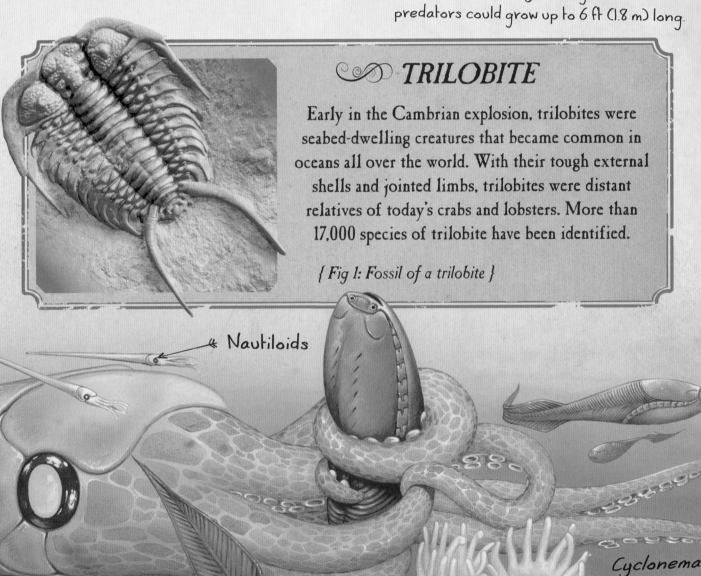

Nautiloids

Cyclonema

Promissum

Strophomena

Rugos corals

EARLY LAND ANIMALS

ABOUT 330 million years ago, forests had extended over most low-lying, moist tropical landscapes. Among the many kinds of four-legged vertebrates living in the forests were early amphibians and reptilelike animals. The wooded areas were also home to giant spiders and insects.

THE COAL AGE

This period of large forests is known as the Carboniferous, which means "coal-making." Remains of the trees of the giant forests of this time eventually became layers of coal in the ground.

Legs of *Dimetrodon* splayed out to the sides of its body, like those of reptiles.

∽ EARLY AMPHIBIAN ∽

This fossil of an early amphibian was found in North America. Amphibians evolved from fish that had simple lungs for breathing air. The first amphibians still spent a lot of time in the water and, like amphibians today, they had to return to water to breed.

{ Fig 1: Early amphibian fossil from Carboniferous period, found in Ohio }

In Permian times,
hunters, such as
Lycaenops (right)
preyed on plant-
eaters such as
Robertia (left) and
Dicynodon (center).

Sharp teeth

PERMIAN TIMES

By 250 million years ago, during a
period called the Permian, the land was
dominated by the ancestors of mammals
and reptiles. The largest animals were
the size of pigs. The giants of the
dinosaur era had not yet appeared.

Rib cage protected the vital
organs in a narrow body.

BREEDING ON LAND

Sail back helped
Dimetrodon to
warm up in the
morning sun.

Unlike amphibians, early land animals
called synapsids could lay their eggs on
land. The synapsids, such as the
meat-eating *Dimetrodon* (left), were
the ancestors of mammals.

ORNITHOLESTES

A swift hunter, *Ornitholestes* lived about 150 million years ago in North America. This dinosaur weighed about as much as a small dog. It may have used its excellent eyesight to hunt at night.

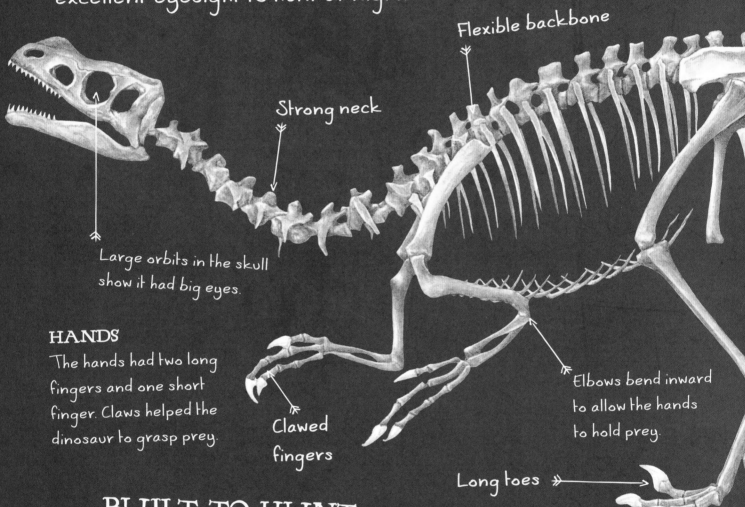

Flexible backbone

Strong neck

Large orbits in the skull show it had big eyes.

HANDS
The hands had two long fingers and one short finger. Claws helped the dinosaur to grasp prey.

Clawed fingers

Elbows bend inward to allow the hands to hold prey.

Long toes

BUILT TO HUNT

Ornitholestes had many features that helped it to catch its small prey. It was fast and agile and ran on two legs. It could use its arms to hold onto prey and had sharp teeth and a strong jaw to bite into it. It had large eyes that gave it excellent vision, even in low-light conditions.

TAIL
The long tail made up more than half the dinosaur's body length.

Tail was held high as it ran.

POSSIBLE PACK HUNTER
Some scientists think that *Ornitholestes* may have been a pack hunter. With its strong jaw and sharp, cone-shaped teeth, it could have joined together with others to bring down larger prey such as young *Camptosaurus*.

LEGS
The bones in the back legs were light, and the toe bones were long and slender. This was perfect for running quickly.

Sharp claws

Misnamed
The name *Ornitholestes* means "bird robber." The dinosaur was once thought to have hunted birds, but we now know that it lived before birds and probably preyed on lizards.

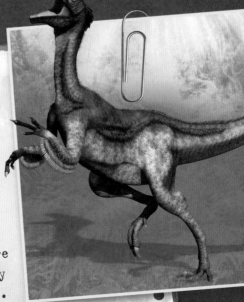

Ornitholestes was about 6 ft (1.8 m) long and weighed 25 lb (11.4 kg).

SMALL PREDATORS

SOME of the smallest dinosaurs were fast-moving, two-legged predators. The smallest dinosaurs of all, such as *Saltopus*, were about the size of a chicken, weighing as little as 2 lb (1 kg).

Feathered body

The birdlike Protarchaeopteryx had feathers but probably could not fly. Its chest, tail and upper legs were covered with downy feathers 1 in (2.5 cm) long.

Clusters of long feathers grew on its arms and the end of its tail.

PREY
These small predators had a varied diet, including lizards, frogs, small mammals and insects.

Short arms »

TURKEY-SIZED DINOSAUR

Compsognathus (right) was a two-legged predator that was built for speed. Like modern birds, it had hollow bones, which made it lighter. It also had a long neck and tail, and long shins suitable for fast running. Its short hands had three pincerlike fingers for grabbing prey.

Strong » claws on both hands

12

{ Fig 1: Skull }

SKULL
Compsognathus had a long, narrow skull, with large sockets for the eyes. It had sharp eyesight for spotting fast-moving prey.

DINO MYSTERY
Very little is known about *Saltopus* as only small pieces of the skeleton have been found.

Small, sharp teeth

❧ WHOLE FOSSILS ❧

Two well-preserved fossils of *Compsognathus* have been found. We know what they ate because the remains of lizards were found in the stomachs of both fossils. *Compsognathus* lived 150 million years ago, and lived on wooded islands and near lagoons.

{ Fig 2: Complete fossil }

GALLIMIMUS

Tail vertebrae

Hipbone

Ribs

Pelvis

THE fast-running *Gallimimus* was an ornithomimid, or "bird mimic" dinosaur. This lightweight theropod probably moved across open plains in groups, searching for food. It had a small head and no teeth, meaning that it had to swallow its food whole.

Long, lightweight legs »

BUILT FOR SPEED

Gallimimus had long legs and short toes that were ideal for running. It held its tail out straight as it ran to stay balanced. Its arms may have been covered in downy feathers.

Short toes »

RUNNING AWAY

Gallimimus had to be on the constant lookout for predators such as the tyrannosaur *Tarbosaurus*. Its best defense was its ability to run away.

Large eye sockets

Shoulder

Neck vertebrae

Toothless mouth

Long, flexible neck supported a small, lightweight head.

BIG EYES

Like ostriches, *Gallimimus* had large eyes, which were placed on the sides of its head, allowing it to spot danger from far away.

SLENDER HANDS

Gallimimus' hands had three clawed fingers, which it could use to pull down the branches of trees to reach the plant foliage.

Claws on each finger

Varied diet

Gallimimus lived in eastern Asia around 70 million years ago. It probably fed mainly on plant material but may also have eaten small animals such as lizards and frogs.

Gallimimus was about 15 ft (4.6 m) long — twice the length of an ostrich.

OSTRICH DINOSAURS

THE long-legged ornithomimids were among the fastest of all the dinosaurs. Like the ostrich, they used their long legs to reach speeds of more than 40 mph (64 kph) and escape predators. The ornithomimids were probably omnivores.

Top sprinter

Of all the ostrich dinosaurs, Ornithomimus had unusually long legs. It may have been the fastest runner of the Cretaceous, reaching speeds up to 50 mph (80 kph).

{ *Fig 1*: Ornithomimus *lived on the plains of North America* }

OSTRICH LEGS

The secret to the ostrich's speed lies in the elastic tendons in its legs, which allow it to spring up as it runs, like a pogo stick. This saves energy, and the bird can run for long distances. The ornithomimids probably had the same bouncy run, and could outlast predators that would eventually tire and slow down.

{ *Fig 2: The ostrich (left) has similar long, muscular legs to the ornithomimid* Struthiomimus *(right)* }

LIGHTWEIGHT RUNNER

Elaphrosaurus (right) was a light dinosaur that lived during the Jurassic period, about 150 million years ago. Many scientists believe that, because of its long limbs and slim body, it was the fastest runner of its day.

STOMACH STONES

Stones called gastroliths have been found in the stomachs of several ornithomimids. The dinosaurs had swallowed the stones, which helped to grind up tough plant matter to digest.

Large thigh muscles powered the long legs.

Skin may have been covered in downy feathers.

Ornithomimids swallowed stones to help their digestion.

17

DROMAEOSAURUS

A small but fierce hunter, *Dromaeosaurus* was heavily armed, with a long, hooked claw on the second toe of each foot, sharp teeth, and a strong bite. It lived in North America about 70 million years ago.

Dromaeosaurus walked on two legs.

Strong muscles in the tail helped to keep it stiff.

STIFF TAIL

The long tail provided balance as the dinosaur ran, just like the tail of a cheetah does today. The dinosaur could sprint at up to 40 mph (64 kph).

Sickle claws

When hunting, *Dromaeosaurus* would leap off the ground to pounce on its prey, tearing at the flesh with the hooked "sickle" claws on its feet.

Dromaeosaurus was about 6 ft (1.8 m) long from nose to tail.

GUESSWORK

A complete skeleton has never been found, so we do not know its exact body shape. Some scientists believe that its body may have been covered in brightly colored feathers.

Birdlike hipbone

Large eye socket

The large head had powerful jaw muscles.

Teeth

TEETH

The teeth curve backward. This allowed the dinosaur to keep a tight grip on its prey.

Rib cage

Long leg bones

Hands had three long fingers tipped with hooked claws.

PACK HUNTER

Dromaeosaurus hunted in packs. A large pack could bring down prey that was much bigger than any of the individual hunters. These hunters had large brains, which they used to help them work together during a hunt.

As it ran, it held its sickle claws off the ground.

DROMAEOSAURS

THE dromaeosaurs were a group of fast, agile hunters that lived all over the world for more than 100 million years. The oldest dromaeosaur fossils date from more than 160 million years ago. The discovery of fossils with featherlike impressions indicate that dromaeosaurs were covered in feathers.

Saurornitholestes

A dromaeosaur that lived in North America about 70 million years ago, Saurornitholestes may have used its claws to dig into burrows and catch mammals.

VELOCIRAPTOR

With one of the largest brains of any dinosaur, the fast-moving, well-armed *Velociraptor* was a danger even to large dinosaurs.

FLYING AND GLIDING

Some scientists believe that a few dromaeosaurs could fly. Fossils of *Rahonavis* show that these dinosaurs probably had the large feathers and strong muscles needed for flight. Other dromaeosaurs such as *Microraptor* may have used their feathered wings to glide from tree to tree.

DEINONYCHUS

A fossil of the dromaeosaur *Deinonychus* made scientists rethink how we see dinosaurs. It was the first dinosaur proven to have been quick and agile, showing that not all dinosaurs were slow animals, as had widely been thought.

{ Fig 1: Like all dromaeosaurs, Deinonychus could quickly rotate its sickle claw to grab hold of its prey }

Protoceratops fights back as the predator tries to kill it.

{ Fig 2: Deinonychus claw }

DEADLY FIGHT

In 1971, a fossil was discovered in the Gobi Desert of a predator fighting with its prey. A *Velociraptor* has its claws around the throat of a *Protoceratops* that is biting the *Velociraptor's* arm as it fights back.

Velociraptor clings to its prey with its hooked claws.

21

IGUANODON

WHEN an *Iguanodon* shin bone was discovered in England in 1809, it was believed to have belonged to a giant mammal. Later discoveries confirmed that it was a dinosaur.

THUMB SPIKE
Iguanodon had a sharp spike on each thumb, which it could use to gouge out the eyes of attackers.

Thumb spike

Five-fingered hands

STRONG LEGS
To support the *Iguanodon's* weight, the leg bones were thick and strong.

Iguanodon could walk on four legs or two.

Hooflike nails

Iguanodon was 30 ft (9.1 m) long and weighed 5 tons (4,500 kg).

Bony tendons crisscrossed the backbone, giving it extra strength.

The tail muscles attached to these spikes and extensions above and below the bones in the tail.

Heavy tail was held straight when the dinosaur walked on two legs.

SUCCESSFUL DINOSAUR

Evidence of *Iguanodon* has been found as far apart as South America and Spitzbergen in the Arctic Circle. It was a very widespread dinosaur. *Iguanodon* was part of the hugely successful group of large plant-eaters known as the iguanodonts.

V-shaped bones gave the tail extra protection.

← Pelvis bone

FOOTPRINTS

Footprints of *Iguanodon* have been discovered in rocks in southern England. These show the animals walking on two legs and traveling in a herd.

IGUANODONTS

THE iguanodonts were heavy plant-eaters that moved around slowly, browsing on shrubs and trees. Iguanodonts reached their peak success around 110 million years ago, when they lived all around the world.

TWO LEGS OR FOUR?

Scientists first thought that iguanodonts walked on all fours like modern-day iguanas. However, it has been discovered that the front limbs were shorter than the rear limbs, and that the tail was stiff and heavy. This means that they could move around just on their rear limbs when they wanted to.

Tall fin on the back may have supported strong muscles.

Probactrosaurus was 18 ft (5.5 m) long and weighed a little more over 1.1 tons (1,000 kg).

SPIKES AND SNOUTS

Probactrosaurus was a plant-eating dinosaur that combined features of iguanodonts and hadrosaurs (see pages 28-29). It had five-fingered hands, which are typical of iguanodonts, as well as a wide, flat snout.

Sarcosuchus, an ancient relative of the crocodile, lived alongside Ouranosaurus.

24

SENSE OF SMELL

Muttaburrasaurus is one of the few dinosaur fossils to have been discovered in Australia. It was similar in appearance to *Iguanodon* but had larger nostrils. It probably relied on its keen sense of smell to find food.

SAIL BACK

Ouranosaurus had a tall, sail-like ridge on its back, similar to that seen on the meat-eating *Spinosaurus*. It is now seen as another dinosaur with iguanodontlike features, such as a thumb spike.

Ouranosaurus drinking at a watering hole.

25

LAMBEOSAURUS

A large, sturdily built dinosaur, *Lambeosaurus* belonged to a group of plant-eaters called hadrosaurs, also known as duck-bills. It used its toothless, horn-covered beak to nip leaves from the ends of plants. *Lambeosaurus* lived in North America about 76 million years ago.

EASY BROWSER

Lambeosaurus moved around on all fours, browsing on low-growing plants. It had a flexible neck with strong muscles, which allowed it to gather food around a wide area without having to move its heavy body too much.

Hollow crest may have been used in courtship display or to make calls louder.

Flat beak was protected by hard horn.

Front legs

Lambeosaurus was
30 ft (9.1 m) long and
weighed 3.3 tons
(3,000 kg).

Birdlike pelvis

Attachments for tail muscles

Heavy tail

GRINDING TEETH

Lambeosaurus had rows of teeth at the back
of its mouth to grind up its tough plant food.
The teeth would wear out and were replaced
with new ones throughout the dinosaur's life,
just like an elephant's teeth do today.

CROUCHING

This skeleton shows
Lambeosaurus on all
fours. It could also rear
up on two legs to run
away from predators.

Thick leg bones

Bony spike points backward from crest.

Hooflike nails on the toes for walking.

DUCK-BILLED DINOSAURS

Corythosaurus tilts its head back to make a loud call.

THE duck-billed hadrosaurs were a very successful group of dinosaurs. They evolved in central Asia but soon spread all across the northern hemisphere, pushing out other plant-eaters such as iguanodonts.

Fossil of a *Maiasaura* chick emerging from its egg.

CARING PARENTS

Hadrosaurs such as *Maiasaura* nested together in large groups. They made their nests by scraping a hollow in the ground, in which they laid their eggs. After hatching, the young could not walk for several months and were fed by their parents.

28

LOUD CALL

The crest of *Parasaurolophus* was a hollow tube nearly 6 ft (1.8 m) long. It may have used the crest like the pipe of a trombone to make its calls much louder. The hadrosaurs could have signaled to one another across large distances with their foghornlike calls.

{ Fig 1: The shape of Parasaurolophus' crest gave it a disctinctive loud call }

Teeth interlock to form a grinding surface.

{ Fig 2: Grinding teeth }

HEAD CRESTS

Many hadrosaurs had hollow crests on their heads. Air circulating through the crests may have cooled the dinosaurs as they fed in the hot sun. The crests also made the dinosaurs' calls louder and may have been used in displays.

CORYTHOSAURUS

Many skulls of the large North American hadrosaur *Corythosaurus* have been found. It had a narrow semicircular crest on its head in the shape of a large fan.

STEGOSAURUS

THE slow-moving *Stegosaurus* was the largest member of the group of plant-eating stegosaurs. It had a small head and a huge body topped with two rows of bony plates. This well-protected dinosaur defended itself with its spike-tipped tail.

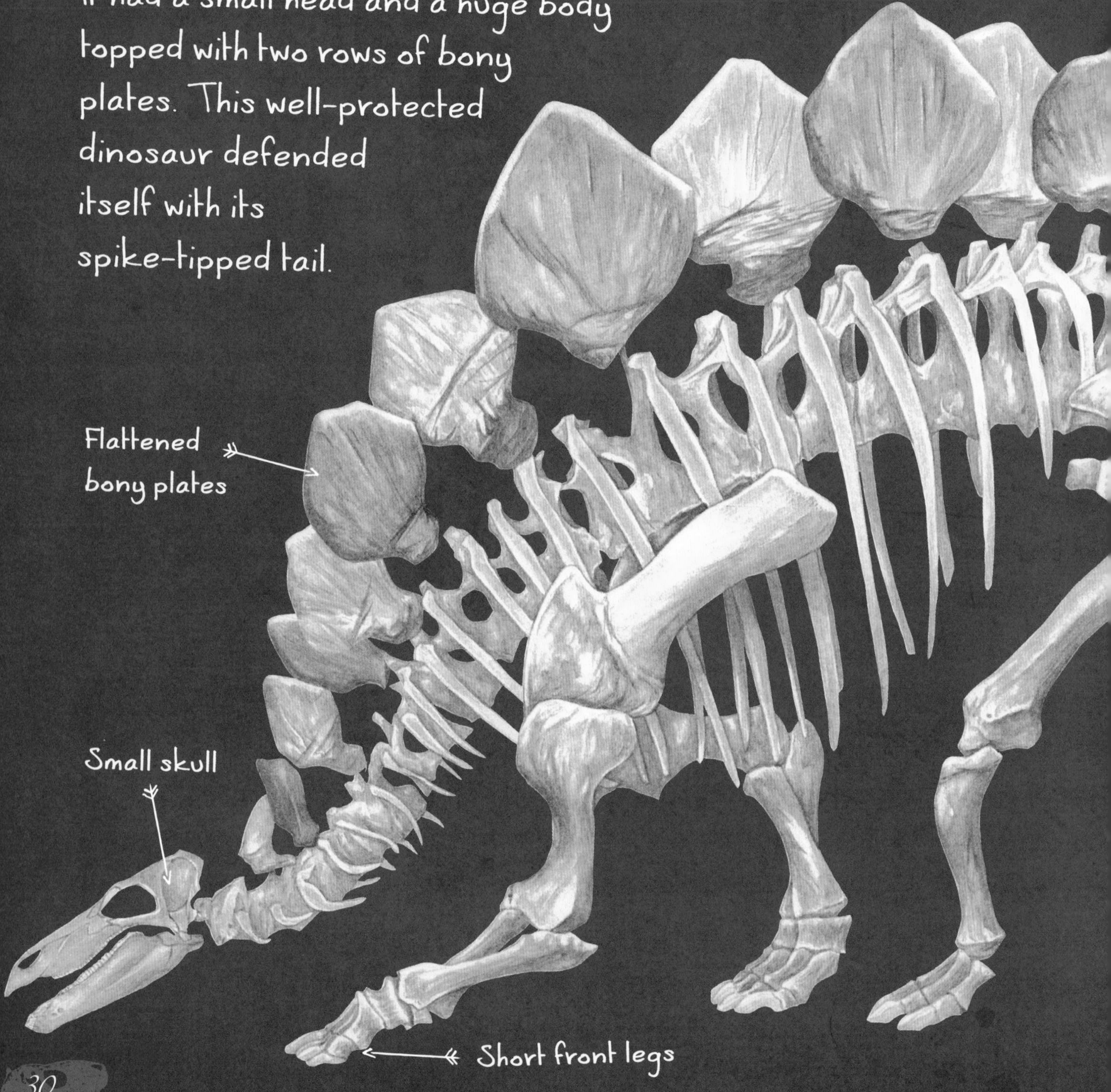

Flattened bony plates →

Small skull →

← Short front legs →

Stegosaurus was more than 20 ft (6.1 m) long.

REACHING LEAVES

Stegosaurus lived in North America about 150 million years ago. It fed on the leaves of the tree ferns of that time by rearing up on two legs.

HEAT CONTROL

The bony plates may have been covered in blood-rich skin. When the dinosaur was cold, it would turn its side to the sun to warm up. When it was hot, it would face away from the sun and lose heat through the plates.

Broad pelvis

STRONG LEGS

Stegasaurus' massive back legs were more than twice as long as its front legs. This allowed it to reach low-lying plants to eat.

Powerful muscles swung the spiked tail from side to side.

Two pairs of spikes

PLATED DINOSAURS

THE stegosaurs were large plant-eaters with small heads and massive bodies. These heavy dinosaurs were well-armored and they usually stood their ground against predators, such as *Yangchuanosaurus*.

TAIL ATTACK

The stegosaurs were slow-moving and had brains the size of a walnut. They could not run to escape danger but would swipe at predators with their powerful tails.

SMALL HEAD

Tuojianosaurus had a skull that was just 15 in (38 cm) long. It protected a tiny brain.

← Tail spikes

SCELIDOSAURUS

Scelidosaurus lived about 190 million years ago and may have belonged to an ancestral group of the stegosaurs. The plates on its back were studded with parallel rows of backward-facing spikes. It used its toothless beak to tear at leaves.

{ Fig 1: Scelidosaurus fossils have been discovered in Dorset in England }

Yangchuanosaurus hunting prey.

JURASSIC DINOSAUR

The stegosaurs first appeared about 170 million years ago. However, by 140 million years ago, most of them had disappeared. Along with most of the giant sauropods, they died out at the end of the Jurassic period.

Large shoulder spines

GIGANTSPINOSAURUS

This medium-sized stegosaur lived in China 160 million years ago. It is named after the two huge spines on its shoulders.

TYRANNOSAURUS

MASSIVE and ferocious, *Tyrannosaurus* was a tyrannosaur — a group of flesh-eating dinosaurs of the Jurassic and Cretaceous periods. Early tyrannosaurs were small, but later ones were bulky animals with powerful jaws and sharp teeth. *Tyrannosaurus* was one of the largest, and fiercest.

LIGHTWEIGHT

Its skeleton was big enough to support the hunter's vast bulk but also light enough to allow it to move quickly to catch prey.

Tail vertebrae

Thigh bone

TAIL BALANCE

Like other dinosaurs that walked on two legs, *Tyrannosaurus* held its long tail straight out behind it. This helped balance the weight of the front part of its body, including its massive head.

Tyrannosaurus was about 40 ft (12.2 m) long and 12 ft (3.7 m) tall.

34

Shoulder blade

Neck vertebrae

BIG HEAD
The massive skull was nearly 4 ft (1.2 m) long, and its monstrous jaws and teeth could rip prey apart in seconds.

Razor-sharp teeth

SHORT ARMS
Tyrannosaurus had surprisingly short arms compared to the rest of its huge body.

Special ribs lined the dinosaur's belly to help strengthen this part of its body.

Two claws on each arm

Lizard ruler
This giant hunter lived in North America some 68 to 66 million years ago, during the Late Cretaceous Period. Translated from Greek, its name means "tyrant lizard."

TYRANNOSAURS

THE tyrannosaurs were huge, two-legged hunters that lived in North America and Asia more than 66 million years ago, during the Late Cretaceous Period.

Tail held out to balance the dinosaur during a chase.

ON THE HUNT

Dinosaur experts have argued about whether tyrannosaurs were hunters or if they simply fed off the dead bodies of other animals. Studies of fossil parts and modern re-creation techniques, however, indicate that this group of dinosaurs actively hunted prey.

{ Fig 1: Hunting vision }

∾ BINOCULAR VISION ∾

Skulls of tyrannosaurs show that these dinosaurs had forward-facing eye sockets. This would have given these hunters good three-dimensional vision, allowing them to judge distances with great accuracy. This feature is usually found in active hunters, such as eagles and tigers.

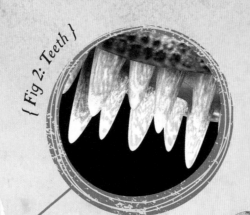

TEETH

The jaws of tyrannosaurs were lined with up to 60 razor-sharp teeth, each measuring nearly 6 in (15 cm).

Prey needed to be nimble to avoid a tyrannosaur's huge jaws.

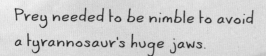

SIAMOTYRANNUS

This tyrannosaurlike dinosaur is now seen as an allosauroid. It lived in what is now Southeast Asia and grew to nearly 23 ft (7 m) long. It may have hunted plant-eaters that were much bigger than it was.

MUSCLES

Tyrannosaurs had powerful muscles attached to the legs and jaw, allowing the creatures to run quickly and then bite with great force.

Lightweight skull

The skull of a tyrannosaur had several large holes. These reduced the skull's weight so that the dinosaur could move it around more easily while hunting prey.

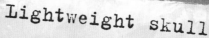

GIGANOTOSAURUS

A huge predator that lived 100 million years ago in South America, *Giganotosaurus* was a fearsome sight. Weighing 7.7 tons (7,000 kg), these meat-eaters had big appetites, and they may have hunted in packs to take down giant sauropods such as *Argentinosaurus*.

Neck moved by powerful muscles.

Hipbone

Narrow jaw

Short arms

Large, sharp teeth

Giganotosaurus was 40 ft (12.2 m) long from head to tail.

NARROW SKULL

Although it was bigger than *Tyrannosaurus*, *Giganotosaurus's* bite was only one-third as powerful. Its narrow skull and lower jaws were adapted to inflict slicing wounds on prey.

Strong feet

CLAWED FINGERS

Giganotosaurus had short but powerful arms. Each hand was armed with three-clawed fingers.

SHORT SPRINTS

Giganotosaurus walked on two legs and could probably sprint at speeds of up to 20 mph (32 kph).

SMALL BRAIN

Inside its narrow head, *Giganotosaurus* had a relatively small brain, which was probably the size and shape of a banana.

Long tail

Giganotosaurus's huge body meant that this massive dinosaur weighed up to 13.8 tons (12,500 kg), about the weight of three elephants.

Bones in the tail

Ankle

Sharp tooth

Giganotosaurus's teeth were up to 8 in (20 cm) long. The teeth were constantly replaced as they wore out. The U-shaped groove at the root of the tooth shows where a replacement tooth was growing.

GIANT PREDATORS

THE carcharodontosaurs and spinosaurs were some of the largest land predators that have ever lived. With their massive jaws, sharp teeth, and claws, they were a terrifying sight to potential prey.

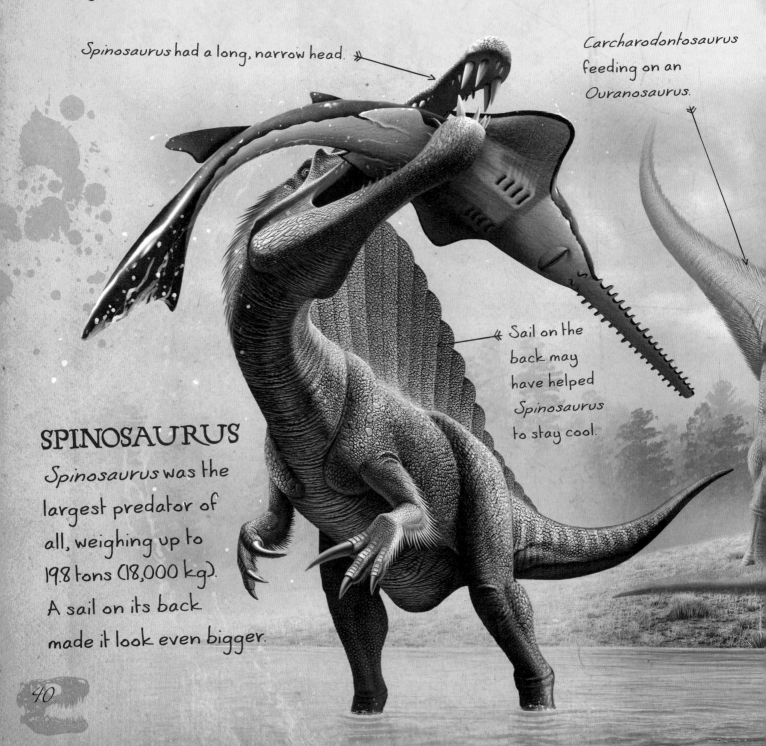

Spinosaurus had a long, narrow head.

Carcharodontosaurus feeding on an Ouranosaurus.

Sail on the back may have helped Spinosaurus to stay cool.

SPINOSAURUS

Spinosaurus was the largest predator of all, weighing up to 19.8 tons (18,000 kg). A sail on its back made it look even bigger.

SHARP TEETH

Carcharodontosaurus was the largest member of the group named after it. Its name means "sharp-toothed lizard." It had long, sharp teeth with sawlike serrated edges. It lived at the same time as the even larger *Spinosaurus*, and it is likely that the two came into conflict with one another.

{ Fig 1: Carcharodontosaurus skull }

FISH-EATER

We know that *Spinosaurus* ate fish, since fish scales have been found in its stomach. This dinosaur may have spent a lot of its time in water, much like modern crocodiles.

Footprints

These footprints of *Acrocanthosaurus* were fossilized in Texas. This carcharodontosaur was 30 ft (9.1 m) long and 3 tons (2,721 kg). It made these prints 115 million years ago.

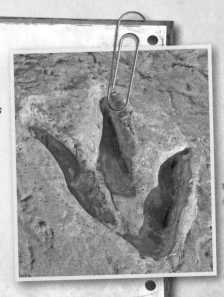

BIG PREDATORS

These carcharodontosaurs are lined up above in size order. From the left: *Carcharodontosaurus, Giganotosaurus, Mapusaurus, Acrocanthosaurus, Eoarcharia* and *Concavenator.*

ALLOSAURUS

THE carnosaur *Allosaurus* lived 150 million years ago. This dinosaur was the largest meat-eater of its time. It may have hunted on its own or worked in packs to bring down large prey such as the giant *Apatosaurus*.

Large, heavy hipbone

AMBUSH HUNTER

Allosaurus preyed on the dozens of species of plant-eaters that lived on the open plains. It was an ambush hunter that would lie in wait for prey such as *Camptosaurus* and pounce on any that strayed too close.

The legs were relatively short, meaning that *Allosaurus* was not a very fast runner.

Allosaurus grew up to 39 ft (11.9 m) long and weighed up to 3.9 tons (3,500 kg).

Hooflike claws on feet

42

SHORT SPRINTS

This predator was too big and heavy to run for long, so it had to catch its prey in short sprints.

Thick neck →

FLEXIBLE JOINTS

The skull bones were joined together loosely, making the skull flexible and strong.

Brow ridges

Lower jaw →

Teeth had sawlike → edges on both sides.

LIGHT SKULL

Allosaurus's massive head was nearly 3 ft (91 cm) long. Openings, or windows, between the skull bones made the head much lighter.

← Broad
rib cage

Three-clawed →
hand

HORNY FOREHEAD

Horny bumps above the eyes may have been used for display or as weapons in battles with other Allosaurus.

EARLY PREDATORS

THE first large meat-eaters appeared on Earth about 200 million years ago. These predators walked on two legs. They had sharp claws and teeth, and a powerful bite.

MEGALOSAURS

The megalosaurs were the earliest of the large predators. These big-boned dinosaurs had powerful jaws and sawlike teeth. They had short but strong arms and three claws on each hand.

Early find

The first dinosaur bone on record was found in England in 1676. It belonged to *Megalosaurus*. Footprints of this mighty predator have been found in limestone rocks.

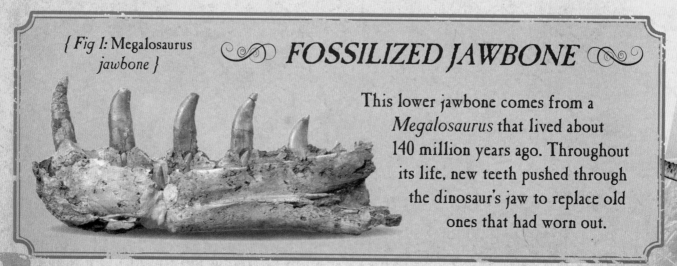

{ *Fig 1:* Megalosaurus jawbone }

FOSSILIZED JAWBONE

This lower jawbone comes from a *Megalosaurus* that lived about 140 million years ago. Throughout its life, new teeth pushed through the dinosaur's jaw to replace old ones that had worn out.

ALLOSAURS

The allosaurs were similar in appearance to megalosaurs but even bigger. They were the largest predators in the Late Jurassic period, 150 million years ago.

PROCERATOSAURUS

Proceratosaurus (above) is known from just one skull. This medium-sized predator lived 170 million years ago. It was an early ancestor of the tyrannosaurs.

Yangchuanosaurus had sharp teeth that curved backward.

YANGCHUANOSAURUS

Bones of the dinosaur Yangchuanosaurus have been discovered in China. It was a large allosaur with a huge head and powerful jaws.

Large, heavy body was balanced by a long tail.

PSITTACOSAURUS

WITH a rounded skull and toothless curved beak, *Psittacosaurus'* name means "parrot lizard." It was a plant-eater and used its strong beak to break off tough leaves and stems.

The beak was also suited to cracking nuts. ⤵

Flexible neck

Short arms ⤵

BLUNT CLAWS
The dinosaur had four blunt claws on each hand. ⤵

HORNY CHEEKS

Psittacosaurus' cheek bones bulged outward into horny projections. In later ceratopids, these would develop into spikes.

Psittacosaurus was 8 ft (2.4 m) long and weighed about 40 lbs (18.2 kg).

WELL KNOWN

More than 400 fossils of *Psittacosaurus* have been found, including several complete skeletons. It is one of the most completely known dinosaurs of all.

→ Birdlike pelvis

Rib cage

← Elbow

HERDING YOUNG

Young *Psittacosaurus* banded together in herds for protection.

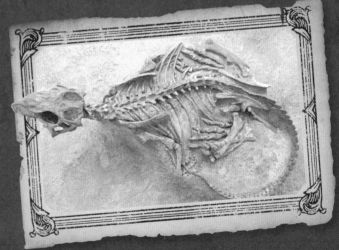

HATCHLING

This fossil of a young *Psittacosaurus* was found in Mongolia. Its body is 5 in (12 cm) long. It died soon after hatching.

Toe bones ↘

EARLY HORNED DINOSAURS

THE HORNED ceratopsians were plant-eaters that thrived across the world. The face horns of early ceratopsians were smaller than the spikes and frills of their later relatives, such as *Triceratops*.

HERD ANIMAL

Like other ceratopsians, *Leptoceratops* (right) lived in herds in upland forests, feeding on small trees and shrubs.

WIDE DIET

With their sharp beaks and grinding teeth, these dinosaurs could feed on a wide variety of plants, from ferns and conifers to flowering plants and trees.

Narrow beak

{ Fig 1: Microceratops }

TINY DINOSAUR

At just 2 ft (61 cm) long, *Microceratops* was once thought to be the smallest horned dinosaur of all. It is now believed that this small fossil was of a young animal, so the name is no longer used. It had long shin bones, which suggests that it was probably a fast runner, able to flee predators.

BAGACERATOPS

The small ceratopsian *Bagaceratops* lived 80 million years ago in Mongolia. It showed some of the features of later frilled ceratopsians, with a short horn on its snout and leaflike horns on each cheek.

Leptoceratops could walk on two or four legs.

Complete fossils

These *Leptoceratops* bones date from 68 million years ago. Although it is thought to be more primitive than *Triceratops*, it lived at the same time as its larger relative.

49

TRICERATOPS

LONG, sharp horns and a bony frill around its neck kept Triceratops safe from the fiercest of enemies. Triceratops was a heavy plant-eater that roamed the forest in search of food.

Backbone has extra vertebrae to strengthen the body.

Triceratops was 30 ft (9.1 m) long, 10 ft (3 m) tall, and weighed more than 8.8 tons (8,000 kg).

Rib cage

Short, thick tail

Thick, strong leg bones carry the weight of its huge body.

THICK LEGS

The thick legs on this dinosaur were strong enough to carry the weight of the creature's huge body and head.

Short, wide toes

CHARGE!

If threatened by a predator, *Triceratops* would charge, just like a rhinoceros, and use its horns as huge daggers to fight off the attacker.

Vertebrae

Neck frill

THREE HORNS

Triceratops' name means "three-horned face." It had two horns on its brow that were up to 3 ft (91 cm) long. It also had a smaller horn on its nose.

Brow horn

Nose horn

Grinding teeth

Beak

Shorter front legs

BEAK

Triceratops had a beak at the front of its mouth that it used to snip off plant material.

FRILLED DINOSAURS

PLANT-EATING frilled ceratopsids such as *Triceratops* were a common sight in the Late Cretaceous Period between 100 and 66 million years ago.

DEFENSE

All ceratopsids were armed with broad neck frills and long, pointed horns. These were found on the enormous heads, which could measure up to 8 ft (2.4 m) long.

The frill protects the neck from a predator's downward bite.

PROTECTIVE RING

Some studies suggest that ceratopsids worked together when threatened to create a defensive ring of horns.

SPIKED FRILL

Styracosaurus was well-equipped to fight off an attacking tyrannosaur. The enormous frill protected its neck and had six large spikes growing out from it. It would also use its long nose spike to rip into the flesh of a predator.

{ Fig 3: Styracosaurus }

BATTLING HORNS

Horns were not just for defense. Male horned dinosaurs may also have used them to battle each other for leadership of the herd. Rivals locked horns and pushed against one another with their neck frills.

MONTANOCERATOPS

The leptoceratopsid *Montanoceratops* had a deep, flexible tail, which may have been waved as a courtship signal. Unlike the more advanced ceratopsids, it had claws on its feet rather than hooves.

Plant-eater

Once a horned dinosaur had snipped off a plant using its beak, it used large teeth in each cheek to chew the food before swallowing it.

ANKYLOSAURUS

BUILT like a tank, the heavily armored *Ankylosaurus* was a formidable opponent to any potential predator. It had a thick skin that was covered with bony plates and had a powerful tail club. This slow-moving plant-eater lived 66 million years ago in North America.

Ankylosaurus was 30 ft (9.1 m) long and weighed about 3.9 tons (3,500 kg).

Hipbones fused to vertebrae

Head spikes

Thick neck

Large nasal cavities inside skull

Flattened rib cage

HEAD SPIKES

Ankylosaurus had a broad head with a blunt snout. A pair of spikes grew out of the back of its head, and another pair grew from its cheeks.

Hooflike claws

FUSED HIPS

To give their bodies extra strength, the massive hipbones were fused to eight of the vertebrae in the backbone.

Lying low

The only way a predator could harm a fully grown Ankylosaurus was to attack its soft belly. But not even a tyrannosaur could tip one over if it crouched down.

SENSE OF SMELL

Ankylosaurus had large nasal cavities inside its skull, giving it a keen sense of smell. It sniffed out its food.

TAIL DEFENSE

Ankyolsaurus could break the bones of an attacker with its tail club, which it would swing sideways. The bones in the tail were connected to one another by thick tendons, making the tail stiff and very strong.

Strong, short legs

Strong tail

Tail club

NO RUSH

Its huge weight and short legs made Ankylosaurus one of the slowest dinosaurs of all. It probably had a top speed of about 6 mph (10 kph).

SLOW-WITTED

With a defensive strategy that involved staying still, Ankylosaurus did not need to do a lot of thinking. Its brain was almost as small as that of Stegosaurus.

ANKYLOSAURS

THE ankylosaurs were very widespread 70 million years ago. They ate tough plant material, nipping leaves and branches off with sharp, horny beaks.

BIG BELLIES

Ankylosaurs swallowed food without much chewing. The tough plant matter was digested very slowly in their huge guts. The size of their guts is the main reason these animals were so big and slow.

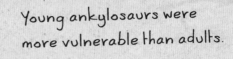

Young ankylosaurs were more vulnerable than adults.

DESERT ANKYLOSAUR

Saichania lived in the hot, dry desert. Its skull was filled with a network of air passages. These helped to cool the air it breathed.

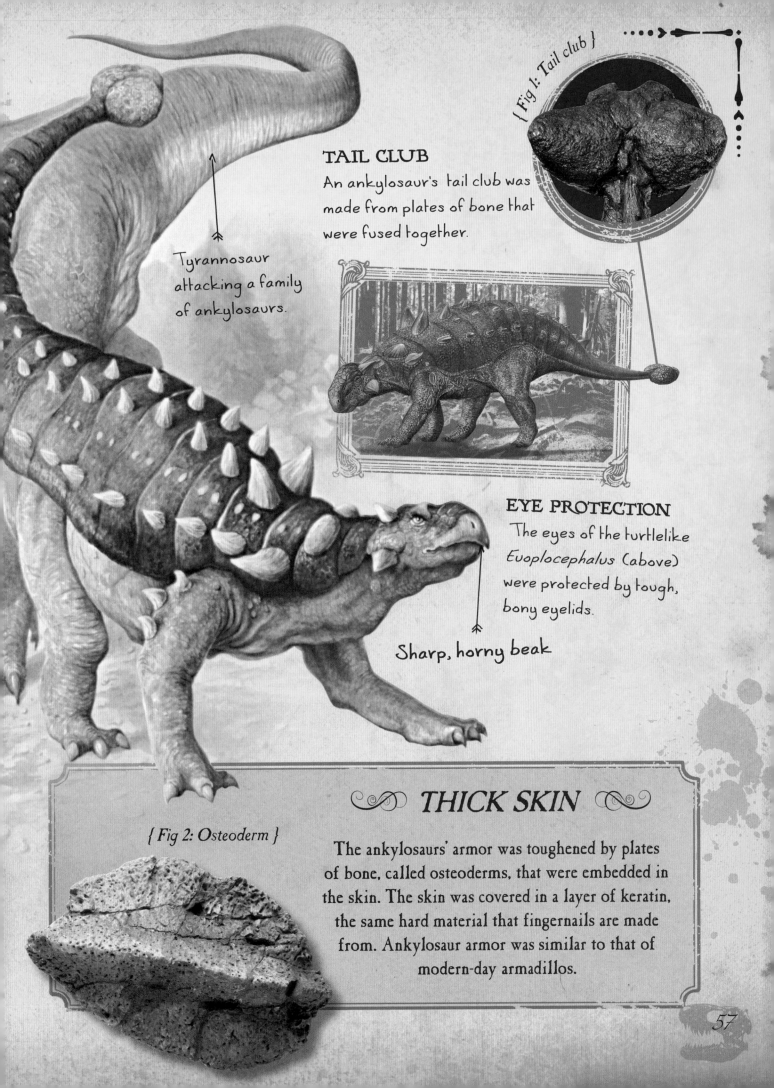

TAIL CLUB

An ankylosaur's tail club was made from plates of bone that were fused together.

Tyrannosaur attacking a family of ankylosaurs.

EYE PROTECTION

The eyes of the turtlelike *Euoplocephalus* (above) were protected by tough, bony eyelids.

Sharp, horny beak

{ Fig 2: Osteoderm }

THICK SKIN

The ankylosaurs' armor was toughened by plates of bone, called osteoderms, that were embedded in the skin. The skin was covered in a layer of keratin, the same hard material that fingernails are made from. Ankylosaur armor was similar to that of modern-day armadillos.

PACHYCEPHALOSAURUS

'THE name *Pachycephalosaurus* means "thick-headed lizard" and the distinctive domed head of this creature was probably used by males when fighting with each other. This was the last of the pachycephalosaurs to become extinct.

RUNNING HERD

Pachycephalosaurus lived in small herds in coastal areas. The whole herd ran away when threatened by a predator. They walked upright on two legs. When running, the dinosaurs held their tails in the air to stay balanced.

Upper leg bone

Heavy, rigid tail

MOUNTAIN GOATS?

Although pachycephalosaurs may have had a similar lifestyle to that of mountain goats today, there is no fossil evidence to support the idea that they lived in mountainous regions.

Pachycephalosaurus grew to 26 ft (9.9 m) long and weighed up to 3.3 tons (3,000 kg).

Broad feet

SOLID BONE

The *Pachycephalosaurus* skull was made of solid bone 10 in (25 cm) thick. This protected its small brain like a crash helmet.

The back was held horizontally while running.

Skull was covered in small knobs.

The neck was short and thick.

Pointed beak

Knee

Five-fingered hands

SKULL REMAINS

Pachycephalosaurus lived in North America. It is only known from its skull, which is 2 ft (61 cm) long, making it the largest of the pachycephalosaurs.

PLANT-EATER

Standing tall on two legs helped the dinosaur to reach vegetation on low tree branches. It had short, sharp teeth that were perfect for shredding leaves and stems.

THICK-SKULLED DINOSAURS

MALE pachycephalosaurs are likely to have used their thick skulls when they battled over breeding rights. Holding their bodies rigid, they would charge and head-butt each other.

Two male pachycephalosaurs engaged in a fight.

Sideswipes could injure the poorly protected flanks.

Strong legs

VICIOUS SIDESWIPE

Their skulls protected the pachycephalosaurs in a head-on clash, but they could also swipe at the soft sides of each other's bodies, as giraffes do.

SPIKY SKULL

The bulbous skull of *Prenocephale* (above) was surrounded by a row of bony spikes, which provided extra protection.

Nearly one-quarter of the skulls of pachycephalosaurs that have been found show evidence of infection. The infection was probably caused by wounded flesh after particularly brutal fights.

Stiff tail

Crown of studs

A *Pachycephalosaurus* skull fossil, showing the crown of bony studs all around its head.

FLAT HEAD

Homalocephale had a thick skull that was flattened on top and dotted with pits and knobs. Some scientists think that it used its flat skull in head-pushing contests rather than head-butting, although many now believe it was actually a young *Prenocophale*.

{ *Fig 1:* Homalocephale *had long legs, meaning that it was probably a fast runner* }

DIPLODOCUS

THE slow-moving Diplodocus was one of the longest animals to walk on Earth. Only very large predators such as *Allosaurus* posed a threat to these sauropods, which lived in herds of small family groups, as elephants do today.

Small head

HIGH NOSTRILS

The nostrils were right at the top of the head. This led some scientists to believe that *Diplodocus* lived in water, breathing with its head mostly submerged. Now, scientists think that the nostrils were there to keep them out of the way of twigs as the dinosaur browsed.

The neck was 20 ft (6.1 m) long.

Diplodocus' vertebrae were partly hollow, which made the dinosaur much lighter.

BIG HEART

To provide enough power to pump blood all the way along its neck to the head, *Diplodocus* needed a big heart. Its heart may have weighed as much as a ton.

Diplodocus was more than 100 ft (30.5 m) long and weighed about 9.9 tons (9,000 kg).

Diplodocus walked on the tips of its toes.

Shoulder
blade

The hipbones were fused
to the vertebrae to give
extra strength.

Leaf-stripper

Diplodocus lived in North
America about 140 million
years ago. It fed on
plants, stripping leaves
from trees with its rows
of small teeth.

LONG TAIL
The tail was made from
more than 70 vertebrae.
Diplodocus carried its tail
off the ground as it walked.

Bones at the
end of the tail
were very thin.

The heavy
body was
supported on
pillarlike legs.

TAIL WHIP
Marks on the bones in the tail show that they
were attached to powerful muscles. *Diplodocus*
would use the tail like a whip, lashing it from
side to side to fend off attackers.

The first toe on each
foot had a large claw.

LONG-NECKED DINOSAURS

THE plant-eating sauropods were the largest land animals that have ever lived. They would use their long necks to browse a large area while standing still.

Neck was made of 19 vertebrae.

DIFFERENT HEIGHTS
With a much shorter neck, *Dicraeosaurus* (above) fed on lower plants than other sauropods.

LONGEST NECK
Mamenchisaurus (left) had the longest neck of all. Its neck was almost as long as the rest of its 70 ft (21.3 m) long body.

BIG BELLIES
To digest the huge amount of food they had to eat, sauropods had giant guts. Like many other plant-eaters, they swallowed stones to help mush up the food inside their stomachs. These stones are known as gastroliths.

LEAF STRIPPER

The bulky *Apatosaurus* (left) lived in North America 150 million years ago. The teeth at the front of its mouth had gaps between them. It used these teeth like a rake to strip leaves from branches.

ARMORED SKIN

The thick skin of *Saltasaurus* (above) was studded with bony plates, giving extra protection against predators.

≪ While some apatosaurs fed, others kept a lookout for predators.

✧ NEW DISCOVERY ✧

The biggest sauropod of all was discovered in Argentina in 2014. It was 130 ft (39.6 m) long, and its thigh bones were longer than a human is tall. This titanosaur lived about 95 million years ago. It weighed more than 77 tons (70,000 kg) — that's as much as 15 elephants.

{ Fig 1: Thigh bone being unearthed }

ANHANGUERA

Anhanguera's long head was twice the length of its body.

Needlelike teeth

Lower beak crest

Eye socket

Short tail

WHEN the dinosaurs roamed the land, flying reptiles called pterosaurs ruled the skies. *Anhanguera* was a kind of pterosaur called a pterodactyloid. Its wings were made from skin that was fixed to long finger bones.

A bone on the wrist helped to control the wings.

DIVING FOR FISH

An expert fish-catcher, *Anhanguera* used its needlelike teeth to grasp hold of its slippery prey. Crests on both its upper and lower beak helped to keep the head steady as it entered the water.

Long fourth finger supported the top edge of the wing.

Anhanguera had a wingspan of 15 ft (4.6 m), but its body was just 8 in (20 cm) long.

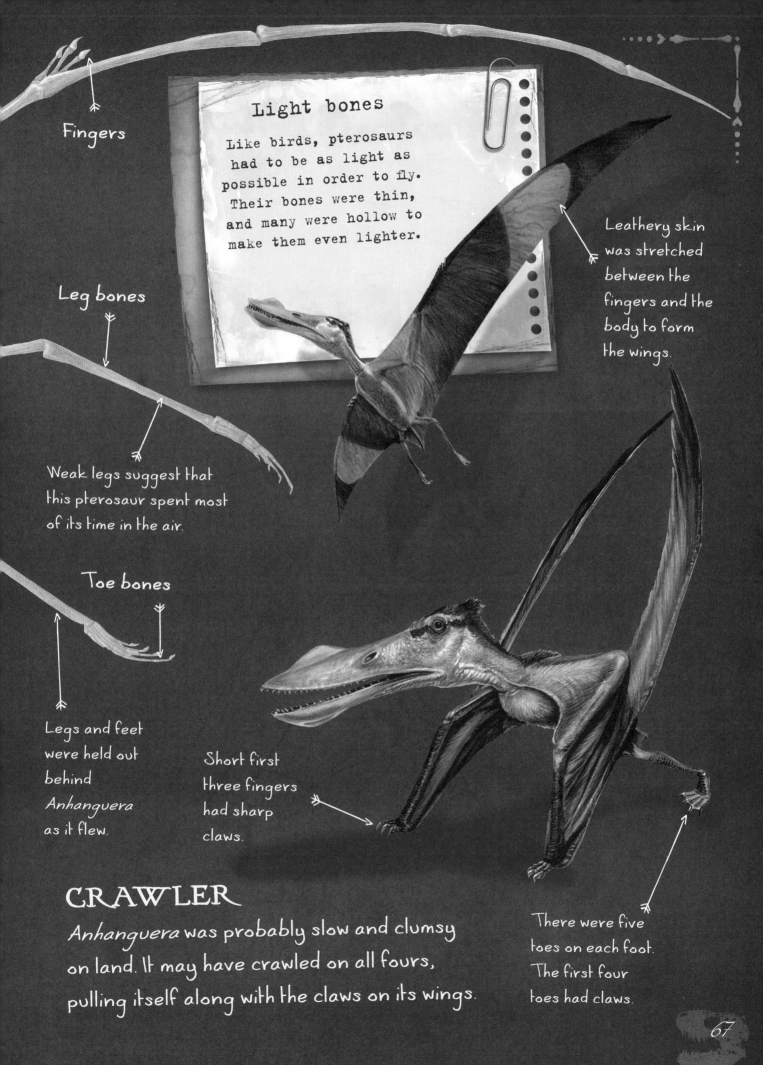

Fingers

Light bones

Like birds, pterosaurs had to be as light as possible in order to fly. Their bones were thin, and many were hollow to make them even lighter.

Leathery skin was stretched between the fingers and the body to form the wings.

Leg bones

Weak legs suggest that this pterosaur spent most of its time in the air.

Toe bones

Legs and feet were held out behind Anhanguera as it flew.

Short first three fingers had sharp claws.

CRAWLER

Anhanguera was probably slow and clumsy on land. It may have crawled on all fours, pulling itself along with the claws on its wings.

There were five toes on each foot. The first four toes had claws.

FLYING REPTILES

THE pterosaurs were the first large animals to take to the air. Before the pterosaurs, only small animals such as insects could fly. They dominated the air for more than 100 million years before dying out with the dinosaurs.

INSECT EATER

Dimorphodon (left) could snap its short beak shut very quickly. It probably used its swift bite to nab insects.

Quetzalcoatlus

The biggest pterosaur was Quetzalcoatlus. It had a wingspan of 36 ft (11 m) — three times the size of the wandering albatross, the largest bird today. This pterodactyloid lived 70 million years ago in North America.

Short tail

CRESTED PTEROSAUR

Tupuxuara lived between 125 and 115 million years ago in South America. This large pterosaur had a flat, rounded crest on the top of its head. The crest was filled with blood vessels, and may have been brightly colored.

Hand bone

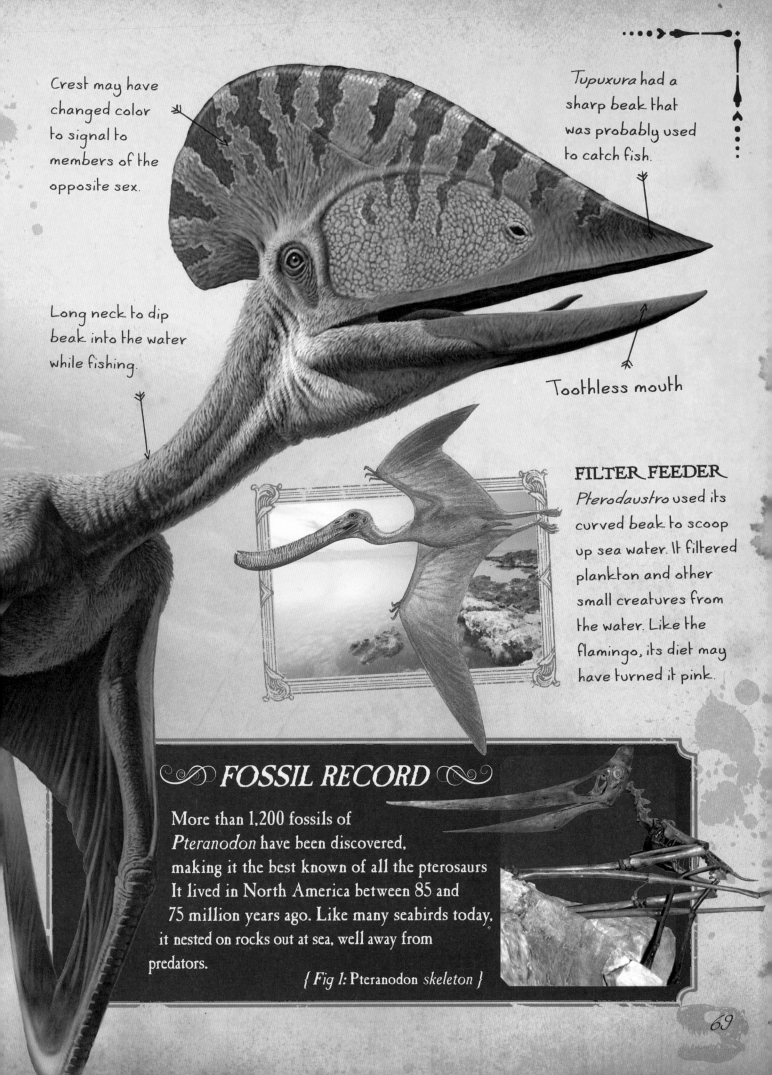

Crest may have changed color to signal to members of the opposite sex.

Tupuxura had a sharp beak that was probably used to catch fish.

Long neck to dip beak into the water while fishing.

Toothless mouth

FILTER FEEDER

Pterodaustro used its curved beak to scoop up sea water. It filtered plankton and other small creatures from the water. Like the flamingo, its diet may have turned it pink.

❧ FOSSIL RECORD ❧

More than 1,200 fossils of *Pteranodon* have been discovered, making it the best known of all the pterosaurs It lived in North America between 85 and 75 million years ago. Like many seabirds today, it nested on rocks out at sea, well away from predators.

{ *Fig 1:* Pteranodon *skeleton* }

OPHTHALMOSAURUS

THE ichthyosaur *Ophthalmosaurus* lived about 160 million years ago. This dolphinlike reptile spent its whole life at sea, even giving birth in the water. Its body was shaped like a teardrop, and it could swim at up to 25 mph (40 kph). It may have used its huge eyes to hunt in the murky water.

Large eye socket was strengthened by a bony ring.

Long, slender, beaklike jaws had no teeth.

Front flippers were strengthened by extra bones.

Ophthalmosaurus was 12 ft (3.7 m) long and weighed nearly 1.1 tons (1,000 kg).

BREATHING AIR

Ichthyosaurs, like dolphins and whales today, had to come to the surface regularly to breathe. *Ophthalmosaurus'* nostrils were at the top of its head, which allowed it to breathe without poking its

FISH DIET

Ophthalmosaurus fed on fish, squid, and squidlike belemites. It caught its prey in its toothless beak and swallowed it whole.

TAIL-POWERED

Ophthalmosaurus pushed itself forward with sideways movements of its powerful tail, which had a broad halfmoon-shaped fin. It used its strong front flippers to steer.

Rib cage

Strong, flexible backbone

End of tail pointed sharply down to support the tailfin.

Rear flippers were small and weak.

Dorsal fin

Born swimmers

Unlike most reptiles, ichthyosaurs did not lay eggs. Instead, they gave birth in the water to live young, like dolphins. The newborn Ophthalmosaurus had to be sufficiently well developed to swim right away.

Babies were born tail-first.

ICHTHYOSAURS

THE ichthyosaurs were large marine reptiles that lived between 250 and 150 million years ago. They had large flippers and streamlined bodies, and they propelled themselves through the water with their powerful tails. Like modern-day dolphins, ichthyosaurs roamed the open oceans feeding on fish.

Large eyes protected by a bony ring.

Unusually for ichthyosaurs, the rear flippers of *Shonisaurus* were as long as the front paddles.

Long, narrow front flippers

SHONISAURUS

The largest ichthyosaur of all, *Shonisaurus* was nearly 50 ft (15.2 m) long. It had long, narrow jaws, with teeth just at the front.

72

SAWLIKE JAW

The upper jaw of *Eurhinosaurus* was twice the length of its lower jaw. Teeth stuck out sideways along the upper jaw, making it a weapon to slash at prey. It may also have used its jaw to probe the seabed for food.

{ *Fig 1*: Eurhinosaurus }

← Sharp teeth

Long, narrow jaws

STENOPTERYGIUS

This small-headed ichthyosaur lived 200 million years ago. Its narrow flippers contained many small bones.

Domed back

Ichthyosaurus

One of the smallest ichthyosaurs at just 6 ft (1.8 m) long, Ichthyosaurus is one of the best known. Hundreds of fossils have been found of this ichthyosaur, which lived 200 million years ago.

BACK TO SEA

Ichthyosaurs were descended from land reptiles that returned to the sea. In the same way, dolphins and whales would later evolve from land mammals that returned to water.

PLESIOSAURUS

ONE of the earliest marine reptiles known as plesiosaurs, *Plesiosaurus* lived nearly 200 million years ago. It was not a fast swimmer but could control its movements very precisely with its large flippers, using its long neck to catch fast-swimming fish.

Sharp teeth

Lower jaw

Long, strong neck

BELLY BONES
Belly ribs joined the shoulder and hipbones to make *Plesiosaurus'* short body rigid and strong.

Searching for prey

Plesiosaurus fed on small to medium-sized fish and squid. It could use its long neck to raise its head high above the water to search for potential prey.

STRONG MUSCLES

The shoulder and hipbones were large and flat. Powerful muscles were attached to the bones to power the flippers.

Plesiosaurus grew up to 11 ft (3.4 m) long.

Long backbone

Flat hipbone

Some scientists think the tail may have had a fin to help the animal steer.

Short tail

Belly ribs

Long flippers

BEATING FLIPPERS

Plesiosaurs swam by beating their flippers up and down through the water, like turtles do today. They used their long necks as a rudder to change direction.

STRONG BONES

Each digit contained up to nine bones, giving the flippers strength and flexibility.

PLESIOSAURS

LIKE their relatives the ichthyosaurs, plesiosaurs were probably fully marine reptiles that had evolved from land reptiles. It is unlikely that such large creatures ever came ashore.

PLIOSAURS

The giant pliosaurs (a type of plesiosaur) were the tigers of the Jurassic oceans. They had powerful jaws and sharp teeth and would prey on sharks, ichthyosaurs, and even smaller plesiosaurs. They had large heads and short necks and were built for speed.

LIVE YOUNG

It was once thought that plesiosaurs dragged themselves ashore to lay eggs, but their limbs could not have supported their weight on land. However, a specimen was found with an embryo in the body cavity, which shows that they gave birth to live young in the water.

The rear flippers were larger than the front ones.

FILTER FEEDER

Cryptoclidus (left) had a jaw full of curved teeth. It fed by gulping water and using its teeth as a sieve. These allowed the water to drain out but left food such as shrimp in its mouth.

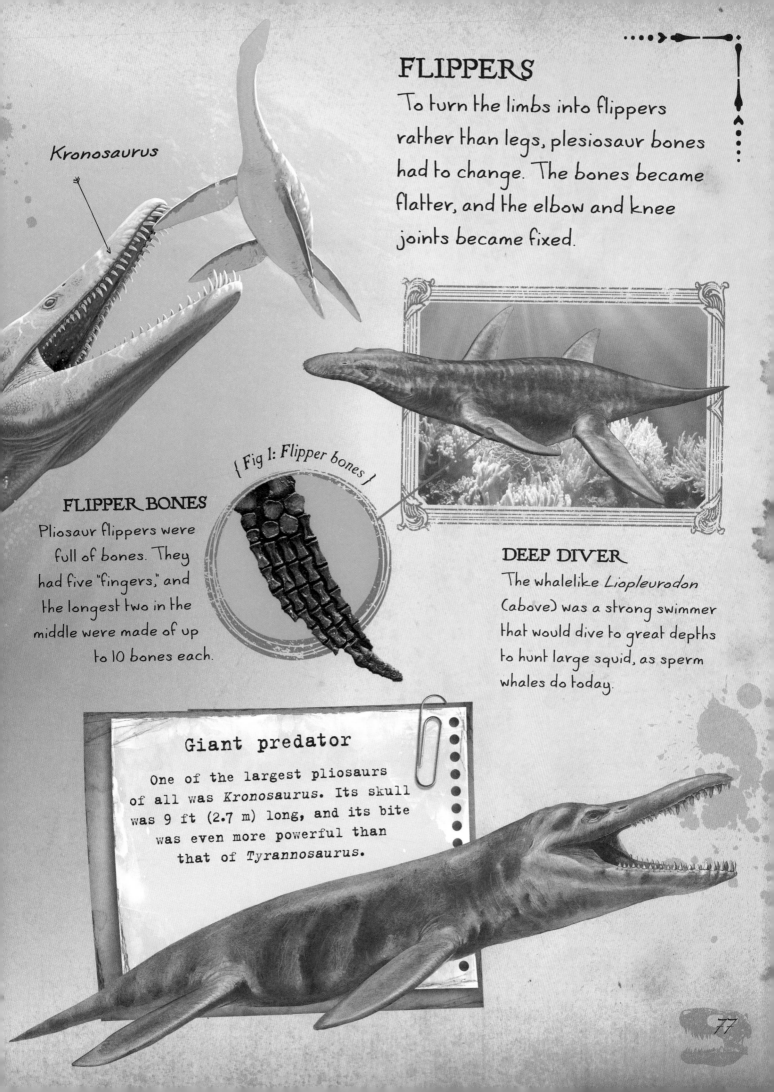

Kronosaurus

FLIPPERS

To turn the limbs into flippers rather than legs, plesiosaur bones had to change. The bones became flatter, and the elbow and knee joints became fixed.

{ Fig 1: Flipper bones }

FLIPPER BONES

Pliosaur flippers were full of bones. They had five "fingers," and the longest two in the middle were made of up to 10 bones each.

DEEP DIVER

The whalelike *Liopleurodon* (above) was a strong swimmer that would dive to great depths to hunt large squid, as sperm whales do today.

Giant predator

One of the largest pliosaurs of all was *Kronosaurus*. Its skull was 9 ft (2.7 m) long, and its bite was even more powerful than that of *Tyrannosaurus*.

ARCHAEOPTERYX

THE earliest known bird, Archaeopteryx, lived in Europe about 150 million years ago. Like dinosaurs, Archaeopteryx had a long, bony tail. The tail was fringed by feathers, which would have helped it to glide through the air.

GLIDER

Archaeopteryx lacked the large breastbone of modern birds, which means that it could only flap its wings weakly. It relied mainly on gliding.

Tail

Long tail was covered in feathers.

TREE CLIMBER

Archaeopteryx was not a strong flier. It would climb trees using its claws and launch itself from a great height. It would then soar through the air in search of insect prey.

Long, thin leg bones

BIRD FEET

The legs were long and thin. Its feet had four toes — three pointing forward and one pointing backward.

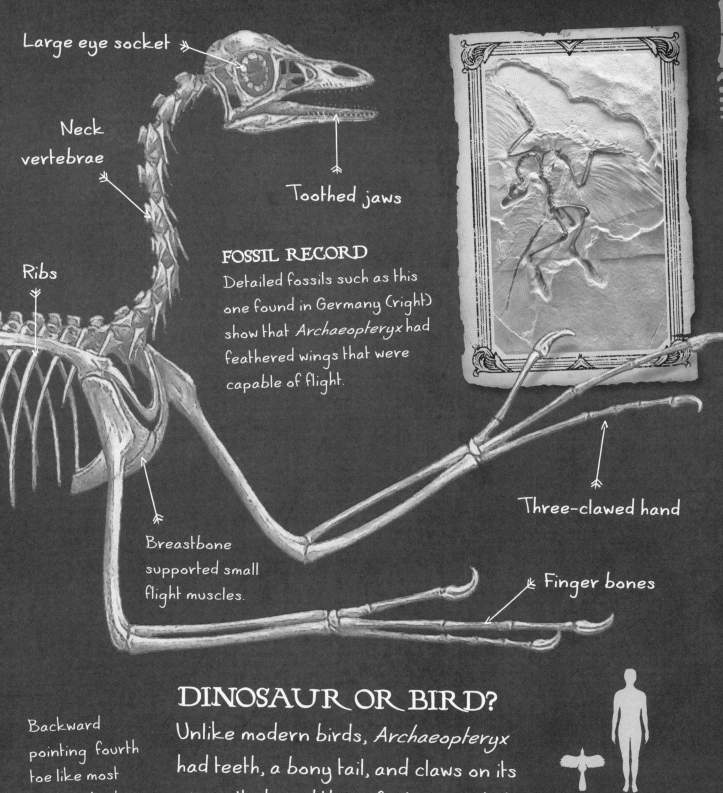

Large eye socket

Neck vertebrae

Ribs

Toothed jaws

FOSSIL RECORD
Detailed fossils such as this one found in Germany (right) show that *Archaeopteryx* had feathered wings that were capable of flight.

Breastbone supported small flight muscles.

Three-clawed hand

Finger bones

Backward pointing fourth toe like most modern birds.

DINOSAUR OR BIRD?

Unlike modern birds, *Archaeopteryx* had teeth, a bony tail, and claws on its wings. It shared these features with the dinosaurs of its time. Scientists think this animal may represent a link between dinosaurs and birds, showing that modern birds have evolved from theropod dinosaurs.

Archaeopteryx was about 14 in (36 cm) long — the same size as a crow.

EARLY BIRDS

ALL of today's birds have evolved from creatures such as *Archaeopteryx*, meaning that birds are the only animals alive today that are directly descended from the dinosaurs. Early birds shared the skies with larger fliers such as the pterosaurs. Over the last 150 million years, many new species of bird have evolved.

Short, thick neck

RUNNING BIRD

Neocathartes seldom flew, and like today's secretary bird, it killed its prey by stamping on its victim with its clawed feet.

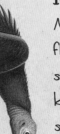

FLIGHTLESS BIRD

Fifty million years ago, one of the largest animals on land was a flightless bird called *Gastornis*. More than 6 ft (1.8 m) tall, this well-armed predator had a huge beak and sharp talons. It was too heavy to move quickly, so it probably caught its small mammal prey by ambushing it.

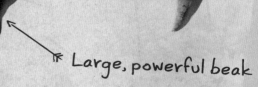

Large, powerful beak

Shrewlike *Leptictidium* being ambushed by *Gastornis*.

BIRDS OF PREY

For the last 50 million years, birds of prey have been widespread. They catch prey with their talons and rip open the flesh with their hooked beaks. *Harpagornis moorei* was a large eaglelike bird of prey with a wingspan of around 10 ft (3 m). It was New Zealand's only large predator and became extinct 300 years ago.

Gastornis had tiny wings that were useless for flight.

Short tail

Seabird

The fish-eating *Ichthyornis* lived 70 million years ago. It was similar to the modern sea tern, except that it had small pointed teeth. *Ichthyornis* was a strong flier that may have traveled large distances.

Broad feet ≫

81

SMILODON

SMILODON was a powerfully built saber-toothed cat that roamed the forests of North and South America until the end of the last ice age, 10,000 years ago. This means that the first human settlers of the Americas would have encountered this fierce predator.

Shoulder blade

Strong neck supported by powerful muscles.

SABER TEETH

The two sabers on the top jaw were serrated on their rear edges, like a steak knife. The teeth would cut through the flesh of *Smilodon's* victims to leave deep, fatal wounds.

Wide-opening jaw.

Saber teeth.

BIG BITE

The jaw could open very wide to allow the cat to sink its huge saber teeth into its prey.

AMBUSH HUNTER

This cat lived in dense forests and bush areas. It relied on surprise to catch its prey, sneaking up and pouncing from close quarters.

Smilodon was 5 ft (1.5 m) long and weighed up to 600 lb (272 kg). It was about the same size as a lion.

Hipbone attached to large muscles, making this cat a good jumper.

LARGE PREY

Smilodon hunted large, slow-moving prey such as bison. It used its strength and weight to knock its prey to the ground before its sabers delivered a deep, cutting throat bite to finish off the stunned animal.

Flexible spine

ROBUST BODY
Smilodon had a more robustly built body than modern cats. It was probably not as swift as lions or tigers.

Legs were short and thick.

Tail was shorter than the tails of most cats.

Broad feet

Sharp claws

LARGE-TOOTHED HUNTERS

EARLY cats were distinguished by their long canine teeth, which were often curved like sabers (a type of sword). Large-toothed cats were once found all around the world, but they had all died out by the end of the last ice age.

SCIMITAR-TOOTH

Homotherium was a scimitar-toothed cat. Its canines were shorter and flatter than those of true saber-toothed cats. Its hind legs were shorter than its front legs, giving it a hyenalike appearance.

❧ FIRST CATS ❧

Catlike creatures first appeared on Earth about 40 million years ago. These animals, such as *Nimravus*, are known as false saber-tooths. Their upper canine teeth were larger than the teeth of modern cats but smaller than the teeth of the true sabertooths, which appeared later. *Nimravus* preyed on birds and small mammals.

{ *Fig 1*: Nimravus }

CAVE LION

The cave lion (right) was the largest cat that has ever lived. It could grow to more than 11 ft (3.4 m) long, and cave paintings show that it was worshiped by early humans. These lions lived in Europe up to about 2,000 years ago.

Teeth were about 6 in (15 cm) long.

Body was built for powerful downward lunges of the head.

Flexible spine allowed the cat to pounce.

Strong legs for short dashes and leaps.

DAGGER TEETH
Megantereon had daggerlike canines and is sometimes called a dirk-toothed cat. It lived between 3 and 2 million years ago in the Mediterranean region.

85

WOOLLY MAMMOTH

SIMILAR in size and appearance to modern elephants, woolly mammoths were plant-eating mammals that lived on the cold tundras of Asia, Europe and North America. They died out at the end of the last ice age about 10,000 years ago.

Woolly mammoths were about 9 ft (2.7 m) tall and weighed up to 5 tons (4,500 kg). Males were larger than females.

Strong, inflexible backbone

Pelvis

Rib cage protected vital organs.

Thick leg bones to support the heavy body.

Wide toes

Domed
head

BIG APPETITE

Woolly mammoths fed on grasses, shrubs, and trees. A large adult needed to eat about 400 lb (181 kg) of food every day, and they may have spent up to 20 hours a day foraging.

Skull was large and strong to support the muscles that controlled the trunk.

TUSKS

Woolly mammoths had long, curved tusks that could be up to 10 ft (3 m) long. They were modified teeth that grew out of the top jaw, and they grew throughout the animal's life.

Four large teeth for grinding food.

FAMILIES

Like elephants, woolly mammoths moved around in family groups led by an old female. Tracks found in Canada show that the younger mammoths had to run to keep up with the big-striding adults.

Staying warm

Woolly mammoths were covered in two layers of fur — an outer layer of long hair and an inner layer of short, dense hair. A layer of fat under the skin helped to keep them warm. They had small ears and a short tail to reduce heat loss.

MAMMOTHS AND EARLY ELEPHANTS

MODERN-DAY elephants are the only survivors of a group called the proboscids. These large mammals had sensitive trunks, which they used to explore the world around them.

Shovel-tusk

Platybelodon spent much of its life wading through shallow rivers. It used the two large teeth on its lower jaw like a shovel to scoop up plants from the water. It died out about 4 million years ago.

ICE-AGE ANIMALS

Mammoths were once widespread across the northern regions. They were well adapted to the cold but died out when the climate warmed.

Tusks were used to clear away snow to get to the plants underneath.

MAMMOTH CALF

Well-preserved remains of woolly mammoths have been found buried in frozen mud in Siberia and Alaska. In 1977, the first complete body of a baby mammoth was found in Russia. Named Dima, he was between 6 months and 1 year old, and died about 40,000 years ago. Patches of chestnut-colored hair remained on parts of the body.

{ Fig 1: Dima the mammoth calf }

Fat was stored in the hump to live off when food was scarce.

DEINOTHERIUM
The lower jaw of the strange-looking *Deinotherium* was curved downward and ended in two large tusks. It may have used its tusks to strip bark from trees.

Pillarlike legs

Large stomach to digest tough plant matter.

Like elephants, mammoths walked on broad toes.

TIMELINE

BELOW we trace the development of life over the last 250 million years. During this time, the face of the planet has changed dramatically, as one giant continent, known as Pangea, split up to form the continents and oceans we know today.

TRIASSIC
252-201 m.y.a.

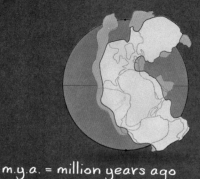

Pangea begins to break up. The first dinosaurs and pterosaurs start to appear.

m.y.a. = million years ago

JURASSIC
201-145 m.y.a.

As new continents form, deserts become rain forests. Giant dinosaurs dominate the land. The first birds appear.

SYNAPSIDS

Shonisaurus

Eurhinosaurus

Plesiosaurus

CROCODYLOMORPHS

Dimorphodon

Stegosaurus

MASS EXTINCTION

The dinosaurs and many other large animals became extinct 66 million years ago. A meteorite collided with Earth, causing a sudden cooling of the climate.

CRETACEOUS	CENOZOIC
145–66 m.y.a.	66 m.y.a.–present day

Today's continents start taking shape. Flowering plants and placental mammals appear.

Following a meteorite strike, the climate cools. The giant reptiles disappear, and smaller mammals and birds dominate in their place.

TORTOISES/TURTLES

MAMMALS

Nimravus

ICHTHYOSAURS

Woolly Mammoth

PLESIOSAURS

Kronosaurus

LIZARDS

SNAKES

TRUE CROCODILES

PTEROSAURS

Pteranodon

ORNITHISCHIAN DINOSAURS

Iguanodon

SAURISCHIAN DINOSAURS

Tyrannosaurus

BIRDS

FOSSILS

WE know about ancient life from fossils. These are the remains of an animal that have been preserved in rocks. Usually, only the hard parts of the body, such as bones, are fossilized, but fossils also include droppings and footprints.

HOW FOSSILS FORM

Most dead bodies do not become fossils. Just occasionally the conditions are right, such as when bones sink into wet mud.

1. A dead dinosaur's flesh is eaten by scavengers.

2. The dinosaur's skeleton lies on the bed of a lake and sinks into the mud.

3. Over time, the sediment covering the skeleton is compressed into rock.

FOOTPRINTS

Sometimes, dinosaur footprints in wet mud have hardened into rock to form fossils. Known as trace fossils, the footprints tell us whether the dinosaurs walked on two or four legs, how quickly they moved, and whether they lived in herds or on their own.

4. Gradually, the bone tissue of the skeleton is replaced by minerals to form the fossil. The land rises out of the water, and the rock is worn away.

Coprolites

Fossilized droppings, called coprolites, tell us what dinosaurs ate. Tiny pieces of bone have been found in *Tyrannosaurus* coprolites, showing how they crunched up their prey.

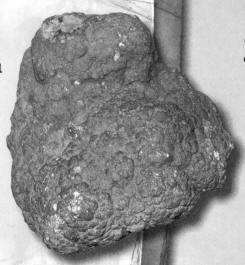

5. The fossilized bones are revealed.

FOSSIL FINDS

Fossils are often found in old quarries, rock debris below cliffs, and anywhere that rock layers have been worn away to reveal the bones.

Pubis

Ischium

{ Fig 2: Ornithischian dinosaur Iguanodon }

∾ DINOSAUR HIPS ∾

After studying their fossilized bones, scientists place dinosaurs into two main groups: the saurischians, or "lizard-hipped" dinosaurs, and the ornithischians, or "bird-hipped" dinosaurs. The main difference between the groups is the shape of the pelvis. In saurischians, the pubis bone points away from the ischium bone. In ornithischians, the pubis bone runs parallel to the ischium bone.

{ Fig 1: Saurischian dinosaur Ornitholestes }

Ischium

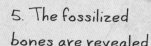

Pubis

GLOSSARY

AMBUSH HUNTER

A predator that hides and waits for its prey to come close before pouncing. Saber-toothed cats were ambush hunters.

AMPHIBIAN

A four-limbed vertebrate animal whose reproduction involves the fertilization of naked eggs laid in water.

BINOCULAR

Vision in which both eyes face forward to focus on the same object. Binocular vision is important to predators because it allows them to judge distances.

CAMBRIAN

A geological period between 541 and 485 million years ago, in which complex animals became widespread in the oceans for the first time.

CARBONIFEROUS

A geological period between 359 and 299 million years ago, in which there was rich plant life in many parts of the world.

CARNIVORE

An animal that only eats meat.

CENOZOIC

A geological era between 66 million years ago and the present day. The era was marked by the expansion of mammals, birds, insects, flowering plants and bony fish.

CRETACEOUS

A geological period between 145 and 66 million years ago. Many dinosaurs lived in this period, which also saw the evolution of birds and mammals.

DINOSAUR

A group of land reptiles that appeared 230 million years ago and became extinct at the end of the Cretaceous. The dinosaurs included the largest animals ever to walk on land, the sauropods.

EVOLUTION

A process of descent from an ancestor brought about by genetic change over generations. The result is that better adapted species replace those that are less well adapted to their environment.

EXTINCTION

The complete dying out of a species of animal or plant. Mass extinctions of many different species can take place when the environment changes suddenly, such as with climate change.

HERBIVORE

An animal that only eats plants. The largest dinosaurs of all, the sauropods, were herbivores.

ICHTHYOSAUR

A group of large marine reptiles that swam using their tails. They did not lay eggs but gave birth in the water to live young.

JURASSIC

A geological period between 201 and 145 million years ago, during which large dinosaurs dominated the land.

MAMMAL

Warm-blooded animals that have hairy bodies. Female mammals produce milk from special glands and use it to feed their young.

METEORITE
A lump of rock that hits Earth from space.

OMNIVORE
An animal that eats both meat and plants.

ORNITHISCHIAN
"Bird-hipped" dinosaurs. This group of dinosaurs were herbivores and included iguanodonts and hadrosaurs.

PANGEA
A giant continent that formed about 240 million years ago and included all the world's land. It started to break up during the Triassic and Jurassic periods.

PELVIS
The bony structure that connects the spine to the hind legs. The dinosaurs are split into two groups according to the arrangement of the bones in the pelvis.

PERMIAN
A geological period between 299 and 252 million years ago. During this period, Pangea formed, and much of the Carboniferous forest was replaced by deserts.

PLESIOSAUR
A group of large marine reptiles that used flippers to swim. Unlike the turtles today, plesiosaurs gave birth to live young at sea.

PREDATOR
An animal that hunts and kills other animals for food.

PTEROSAUR
A group of flying reptiles. Pterosaurs' wings were made of a thin membrane of skin, like the wings of bats.

PREY
An animal that is hunted by a predator.

REPTILE
A group of animals that have scaly skin and mostly lay eggs covered by a shell or membrane. Dinosaurs, ichthyosaurs, and pterosaurs were all reptiles. Modern-day reptiles include crocodiles and lizards.

SAURISCHIAN
"Lizard-hipped" dinosaurs. This group of dinosaurs included plant-eating and meat-eating dinosaurs, such as tyrannosaurs and sauropods.

SCAVENGER
An animal that feeds on the remains of animals that have died naturally or have been killed by predators.

SPECIES
A group of living things of the same type. Members of the same species are very similar to one another and can breed and produce fertile offspring.

SYNAPSID
A group of animals that includes mammals and their reptile ancestors that dominated the land in the Permian period.

THEROPOD
A group of saurischian dinosaurs that were primarily meat-eaters. Today's birds evolved from theropod dinosaurs.

TRIASSIC
A geological period between 252 and 201 million years ago, during which the first dinosaurs appeared on Earth.

VERTEBRATE
An animal with a backbone. The backbone is a row of bones, called vertebrae, that connects the head to other parts of the body. Mammals, fish, birds, reptiles and amphibians are all vertebrates.

INDEX

allosaurs 42–43, 45
amphibians 8
Anhanguera 66–67
ankylosaurs 54–57
apatosaurs 65
Archaeopteryx 78–79, 80
beaks 22, 46, 49, 51, 56, 57, 80, 81
binocular vision 36
brains 20, 32, 39, 55
Cambrian explosion 7
Carboniferous 8
carcharodontosaurs 40–41
carnosaurs 42–43
cave lions 85
ceratopsians 48–53
club tails 54, 55, 57
Compsognathus 12–13
coprolites 93
Corythosaurus 28–29
crests 26, 27, 29, 68, 69
Cretaceous 34, 35, 36, 91
Deinonychus 21
Deinotherium 89
Dimetrodon 8–9
Diplodocus 62–63
dromaeosaurs 18–21
duck-billed dinosaurs 26–29
eggs 9, 28
elephants, early 88–89

eyes 10, 13, 15, 57, 70, 79
feathers 12, 17, 19, 78–9
fighting 21, 53, 58, 60–61
flight 20, 66–69, 78–81
flippers 70, 71, 72, 75, 76, 77
footprints 23, 41, 92
fossils 5, 13, 44, 49, 69, 79, 92–93
frilled dinosaurs 50, 51, 52–3
Galliminus 14–15
Gastornis 80–81
gastroliths 17
Gigantosaurus 38–39
gliding 20, 78
guts 17, 56, 64, 89
hadrosaurs 24, 25, 26–27
hands 10, 15, 19, 22, 24, 39
head spikes 54
hearts 62
heat control 31, 40, 56
herds 23, 47, 48, 58, 62, 92
hips 54, 63, 83, 93
hollow bones 12, 67
Homotherium 84
hooves 22, 27, 42
horned dinosaurs 48–53
Ichthyornis 81
ichthyosaurs 5, 70–73

iguanodonts 22–25, 28
jaws 37, 44, 73, 82
Jurassic 33, 34, 45, 90
Kronosaurus 77
Lambeosaurus 26–27
Leptoceratops 48, 49
Maiasaura 28
mammoths 86–9
marine reptiles 70–77
mass extinction 5, 91
megalosaurs 44
Megantereon 85
Microceratops 49
Montanoceratops 53
muscles 17, 24, 37, 75, 83
nests 28
Nimravus 84
nostrils 62, 70
Ophthalmosaurus 70–71
Ornitholestes 10–11
ornithomimids 14–17
pachycephalosaurs 58–61
Parasaurolophus 29
pelvis 27, 47, 93
Permian period 9, 90
Platybelodon 88
plesiosaurs 5, 74–77
pliosaurs 76–77
Proceratosaurus 45
Protarchaeopteryx 12
Psittacosaurus 46–47
pterosaurs 66–69, 80
Quetzalcoatlus 68
reptiles, early 8, 9
saber teeth 82, 83, 84, 85

sail backs 24–25, 40
sauropods 33, 62–65
Scelidosaurus 32
Shonisaurus 72–73
skin 57, 65
skulls 13, 35, 37, 38, 43, 52, 59, 60–61
Smilodon 82–83
Spinosaurus 40–41
stegosaurs 30–33
Styracosaurcarus 53
teeth 9, 27, 29, 34, 37, 39, 41, 43, 44, 49, 65, 82–85
therapods 14, 79
thumb spikes 22, 25
timeline 90–91
Triceratops 48, 49, 50–51
trilobites 7
trunks 88
Tupuxuara 68–69
tusks 87, 88, 89
tyrannosaurs 34–37
Velociraptor 20–21
vertebrates 8
wings 66–69, 78–81
woolly mammoths 86–87
Yangchuanosaurus 33, 45
young 9, 28, 47, 70, 71, 76, 88